S0-DXN-899

Children's Sermons
for Special Times

CHILDREN'S SERMONS
for
Special Times

C.W. BESS

BROADMAN PRESS
Nashville, Tennessee

© Copyright 1988 • Broadman Press
4249-29
ISBN: 0-8054-4929-9

Dewey Decimal Classification: 252.53
Subject Heading: CHILDREN'S SERMONS
Library of Congress Catalog Card Number: 87-36466

Printed in the United States of America

Library of Congress Cataloging-in-Publication Data

Bess, C. W., 1942-
  Children's sermons for special times / C.W. Bess.
    p. cm.
  ISBN 0-8054-4929-9 :
  1. Children's sermons.   I. Title.
BV4315.B48   1988
252'.53—dc19   87-36466

*To the children
of Central Baptist Church*

Acknowledgments

This book represents a team approach beginning with the children of Central Baptist Church in Jacksonville, Texas. Each Lord's Day they swarm around me at the altar during their special time in morning worship. Because they patiently tested every idea and sometimes changed the children's sermon direction, this is their book dedicated with a pastor's love.

Mary, my ministering mate at home, encourages me in these many writing projects which demand daily discipline and old-fashioned homework at night. Also at home are two other avid supporters, son Craig and daughter Kristen. Their subtle hints keep me going. "Dad, my personal bookshelf needs another book from you this year. Shouldn't you be working on one tonight?"

Other team members include Gina Ginsel, my secretary and professional partner in these annual projects. Gina quickly turns dictated tapes into readable manuscripts. No secretary could be more efficient or helpful.

Every completed manuscript needs careful proofreading. Anne Hall reads the preliminary draft while Anne Hendry combs the final copy for those elusive mistakes and vague phrases which need clarification. I appreciate them serving on my team yet again.

Finally, I acknowledge the support of my congregation. For over a decade now these Central Baptist saints have encouraged me to share my local ministry nationwide through the printed page.

Contents

Part I
Sermons for Holy Days
and Holidays

New Year's Day
Valentine Day
Easter Season
Mother's Day
Memorial Day
Father's Day
Independence Day
Halloween Season
Thanksgiving Season
Christmas Season

New Year's Day

The Lifesaver

Visual Introduction: A roll of candy Lifesavers hidden in a sack.

Sentence Summary: Jesus is our Lifesaver.

Scripture Text: "The saying is sure and worthy of full acceptance, that Christ Jesus came into the world to save sinners" (1 Tim. 1:15).

This is the first children's sermon of a new year. Before I show you children what is inside this sack, consider this child's riddle. "If you know the world is about to end, and you have less than a dollar to spend, what should you quickly buy?"

If you cannot solve that riddle, let me pull something out of my sack which will cost less than a dollar. It is a roll of candy Lifesavers!

Of course, that is only a clever little riddle. Candy cannot save anyone from dying. But these popular and colorful little circles of candy remind us of flotation rings commonly found on ships and boats. If you fall overboard, someone will see you in the water (We hope!) and grab that flotation device off the wall. Your friend throws it into the water close to you. It floats, so you grab hold and hang on for dear life. Saved by a lifesaving ring. But that person who threw the floating ring is also your lifesaver.

Jesus came into the world to be our Lifesaver. We need to be saved because we are sinners. Only Jesus can save us. He is our Lifesaver. Without Jesus we are doomed just as surely as if we were drowning.

Paul reminded Timothy that Jesus came to be a Lifesaver who saves sinners like us. "The saying is sure and worthy of full acceptance, that Christ Jesus came into the world to save sinners" (1 Tim. 1:15).

That is the ageless lesson we must teach every year. It is an old truth for a new year. Jesus is our Lifesaver. He came from heaven into this world for that purpose. He wants to save us because He loves us.

New Year's Day

Plan Now!

Visual Introduction: Appointment book or calendar.
Sentence Summary: Plan your time to include the best things.
Scripture Text: "So teach us to number our days/that we may get a heart of wisdom" (Ps. 90:12).

Here is a new calendar to remind us that we are beginning a new year with many new opportunities. It will likely be another busy year.

Have you ever noticed that every day becomes filled with too many things to do? We stay busy all the time, yet we cannot do it all. We can be in only one place at a time. That is why this little book or calendar is so helpful. It has every day of the week and month listed in plain sight. We have room to write down all the important things we want to do for each day. This is called an appointment book. Most people use a regular calendar for the same purpose.

A calendar helps us to realize that we have only seven days a week. If we want to do something important, like take a vacation or go visit grandparents, we must plan in advance. So we write it down on this calendar for the new year.

Perhaps your parents want you to keep your room clean. To remind you of this duty, they ask you to schedule it on your calendar. So you write a note on each Saturday. "Clean my room!" That helps you plan your time for chores and still have time for fun.

Long ago Moses realized how important good planning is. We must count our days carefully. Here is what Moses said in a poem which became Psalm 90:12. "So teach us to number our days/that we may get a heart of wisdom." We won't live forever here on earth. Best count your days carefully. Be wise in your heart, and plan all the best things that you want done. That will help make a new year happy.

Valentine Day

God's Love

Visual Introduction: Valentine card or any heart symbol.
Sentence Summary: God proved His love to us on the cross.
Scripture Text: "But God shows his love for us in that while we were yet sinners Christ died for us" (Rom. 5:8).

Here is a Valentine Day card complete with a pretty red heart on the cover to symbolize love. Millions of Valentine Day cards like this will be bought and given during this season because people want to express their feelings to those they love. But what is love? Perhaps we should spend a few moments thinking about real love.

When a boy gets a crush on a sweet little girl, we adults joke about it being a case of puppy love. You know why? Because we worry that puppy love leads to a dog's life!

Perhaps you didn't understand that joke, but your parents did. Here is how a ten-year-old explained his feeling of love represented by this red heart.

> Love is a funny thing;
> It's just like a lizard.
> It curls up round in your heart,
> And jumps in your gizzard!

That boy's father had his own poem:

> Love is like an onion:
> We taste it with delight.
> But when it's all gone,
> We wonder what made us bite!

Now those are funny ways to explain love, but the Bible

points us in a better direction. It teaches us that God gave the best example of love. More than just saying "I love you" or even sending a card about love, God showed us His love by dying for us on a cross. In Romans 5:8 we learn "But God shows his love for us in that while we were yet sinners Christ died for us."

That means God loved us before we ever started loving Him. He did not wait for us to become pretty or nice to love us. While we were still sinners, He showed His wonderful love by dying on the cross.

I'm going to draw something on this Valentine Day card which helps explain God's love. Watch now as I draw the sign of a cross. The next time you see a valentine, think about the cross. That's how God proved His love to us.

Easter Season

Joy in the Morning

Visual Introduction: Onion
Sentence Summary: No matter how sad we feel now, we will soon be happy again.
Scripture Text: "Weeping may tarry for the night,/but joy comes with the morning" (Ps. 30:5c).

Here is an onion. Surely you know what happens when someone slices this onion with a knife. That person starts crying.

No, it is not because slicing an onion is such a sad duty. There is a good explanation why we get tears in our eyes from these onions. You see, onions are very juicy inside. A knife slicing through an onion causes a thin spray of onion oil to spread in the air. Then these small drops of onion juice drift into our eyes where they cause an irritation. This does not really hurt, but the eye fills with tears trying to wash out that onion spray.

Don't worry. When an onion causes you to cry, it will only be temporary. This kind of weeping does not last long.

Come to think of it, none of our tears last long. We don't cry forever, do we? Perhaps you stumble and hurt your knee. You cry some great big tears. But after a little while, it feels better. Then you stop crying.

Long ago King David recognized this truth. In Psalm 30 he said that "Weeping may tarry for the night,/but joy comes with the morning." Many centuries later that truth was best demonstrated at the first Easter season.

Mary wept as her Son Jesus died. Peter wept bitterly. So did other devoted disciples. Although it was only midday, the sky grew dark as night for three hours. What a long fearful darkness fell over those followers of Jesus.

Yet it was a temporary time. On that first Easter Jesus appeared alive. They forgot their tears and became happy again. The night of crying passed. Joy came in the morning.

So the next time you cry because you feel sad or hurt, just remember that things will be better tomorrow. Tomorrow you will be happy.

Easter Season

Always the Same

Visual Introduction: Easter lily.
Sentence Summary: Jesus is always the same regardless of the season.
Scripture Text: "Jesus Christ is the same yesterday and today and for ever" (Heb. 13:8).

Today is Easter. It seems that everyone wants to be in church on this special Sunday. So this is a good day to begin a new routine of attending church every Sunday!

We also see many new spring suits and Easter bonnets. Spring is the season when we change from our heavy winter clothing into something lighter and brighter. Many people buy new clothes for Easter.

But you are wondering about this Easter lily which I'm holding. It reminds us of the new season. Outside all nature seems so fresh and new.

This Easter lily is a picture of our new hope which we have in this season of resurrection. Flowers, grass, and trees which seemed dead during the winter have come alive once again. They are so new.

One thing, however, we must admit is not new. Jesus is not new. Just because we have a new season is no reason to expect a new Jesus. The Bible says that Jesus never changes. He is always the same. That is why He would not stay dead when mean people killed Him on the cross. People have no power to change God.

So in the midst of much which seems new let us remember this verse: "Jesus Christ is the same yesterday and today and for ever."

Easter Season

Mystery

Visual Introduction: Large cardboard cutout of a question mark.

Sentence Summary: God reveals some mysteries to little children.

Scripture Text: "At that time Jesus said, 'I praise you, Father, Lord of heaven and earth, because you have hidden these things from the wise and learned, and revealed them to little children' " (Matt. 11:25, NIV).

Here is a symbol which everyone understands. But if you do not understand what this means, just shrug your shoulders and raise your eyebrows as if you want to question this matter. You see, that's what this symbol means— a question.

Think of it as a mystery. Anything we don't understand is a mystery. Even if we are very wise and have learned the secrets of many mysteries, we cannot understand everything.

When we go to school, we expect the teacher to know more than we do. But very often the teacher will have to say, "I don't know the answer to that question. I am just like you children. It is a mystery to me."

Yes, we adults are supposed to be smart. We know more about life and the meaning of big words than you children know. But sometimes we can't understand the most valuable things in life like trust and faith. Yet the greatest mystery of all is death. What is it like to be dead and then come back alive?

Once Jesus prayed to the Father God in heaven, thanking Him that He had hidden many mysteries from the wise people but revealed them to the little children. Listen as I read that verse in Matthew 11:25.

That's an exciting thought. Some mysteries you children understand better than we adults. On another occasion Jesus told the adults that they ought to become like little children because children understand feelings of trust and faith better than the adults.

When the Bible says Jesus died and came back alive, you children seem to accept it better than we adults. While it remains a mystery to everyone, we're glad that at least the children have faith to simply believe this mystery.

Easter Season

It Is Finished

Visual Introduction: Tire pump and flat tire on bicycle wheel.

Sentence Summary: Instead of doing a job only halfway, finish it like Jesus did.

Scripture Text: "It is finished" (John 19:30).

Today I have brought along the front wheel of my bicycle. Notice that the tire is flat. All the air has slowly leaked out through a tiny hole caused by a thorn.

It is good exercise to ride a bicycle in pretty weather. But not with a flat tire! Recently it seemed that every time I wanted to ride, my front tire was flat. So I had to get out the tire pump and inflate the tire to the proper level.

But next time the tire would be flat again. So again I would have to pump the flat tire full. This didn't take long, but it was really a bother. The task was never finished.

Would it not be easier just to take time and fix the tire? Yes, but I could never find a convenient time. I was too busy. I kept promising myself that maybe next time I could fix the tire right.

Now that's foolish, isn't it? If a job is worth doing at all, it is worth doing right the first time. Then it is finished.

In this Easter season, we celebrate a victory which is forever final. When Jesus came to live and die for us, He didn't do it only halfway. He finished the job. He went all the way to death and beyond. On the cross His dying words were truly spoken: "It is finished." While Jesus returned to life three days later, it was His death on the cross that completed the necessary payment for sin. "It is finished"!

Mother's Day

A Mother Always

Visual Introduction: Mother's Day card.
Sentence Summary: While children may grow to be adults, they will always remain children to both God and mother.
Scripture Text: "For ye are all the children of God by faith in Christ Jesus" (Gal. 3:26, KJV).

This is Mother's Day, a special time when we give honor and respect to mother. Everyone of us begins life on earth with a mother. We cannot be born on earth except through a mother's body. That is God's plan.

If a woman follows God, she can become a very special person through motherhood. Mothers deliver us in birth, feed us, diaper us, and help us to grow up into strong adults. No matter how famous we may become, no matter how important or strong, we still remain a child to the mother who loves us.

The most famous man in all of Europe during the 1800s was Napoleon Bonaparte. With the French armies behind him, he conquered all of Europe and declared himself emperor. That's like a king. Emperor Napoleon decided that no one could enter his presence without first kissing his hand. That was the old way that people showed their respect for a king. Because people were afraid of Napoleon, they would bow and kiss his hand.

But one woman refused to kiss his hand, even when he extended it to her. She slapped his hands very hard and told the famous general that to her he was still just a mere child. Do you know who that woman was? Of course you do. That was Napoleon's own mother who reminded him that she had raised eight children—and he was just one of the eight.

That was a very good lesson for Napoleon to learn. We are always someone's child. The Bible teaches us that God looks upon us as little children. The best thing we can do is to become children of God. That happens when we trust Jesus Christ as Savior. We are born again and become like little children. "For ye are all the children of God by faith in Christ Jesus."

Memorial Day

Let Us Remember

Visual Introduction: String on finger.
Sentence Summary: Don't forget that Jesus died for us.
Scripture Text: "Do this in remembrance of me" (1 Cor. 11:24).

Oh me! Have I forgotten something? I have the feeling that I was supposed to remember something. Earlier today I tied this string on my finger.

Yes, I remember now. I tied this string on my finger to remind me to stop by and visit a patient in the hospital today. Now I am glad that I tied this string on my finger. It did the trick. It helped me remember something important.

We have many little reminders in life. Some people write a note on paper and then tape it to the bathroom mirror. Then next morning when they start to brush their teeth, they look in the mirror and see the note. That way they can remember something important. I saw a bumper sticker recently. It simply said: "Don't Forget to Vote." Because it was on the bumper of a car in front of me, I remembered to vote.

Today is Memorial Day, a national holiday set aside to remember those who have died in service to our country. We have this day marked on all calendars as a sort of reminder to remember the dead. Many families visit the cemeteries where they place flowers on the graves of loved ones. We also remember those who died in war defending our country.

Long ago Jesus died on the cross for us. We must never

forget that fact. To help us remember, Jesus left us with something by which we could remember Him.

The Lord's Supper is our reminder. We eat the bread and drink from the cup to help us remember how Jesus gave His body and shed His blood for us.

Jesus said, "Do this in remembrance of me."

Father's Day

Whose Are You?

Visual Introduction: Identification cards.
Sentence Summary: Who you are depends upon whose you are.
Scripture Text: "We are the Lord's" (Rom. 14:8).

For our interest objects today several people have provided these different cards and pieces of paper. Here they are in my hand all mixed up. But I know who owns each card because each has a name on it.

These are identification cards which identify a person by name. Most common is the driver's license which has both a name and picture on it. Another is a student identification card from a local school.

Notice that these cards tell not only who we are but to whom we belong. If my driver's license is issued by California, then I am a citizen of the state of California.

If you have a dog or cat, perhaps that pet has a name tag worn around the neck. It may say "Fido." More important than Fido's name, however, is the name of his master. Fido's dog tag ought to tell not just who he is but to whom he belongs. Every dog ought to belong to someone.

A church secretary told the pastor, "A little boy is here who wants to see you. He did not tell me his name, so I do not know *who* he is. But his red hair causes me to think I know *whose* he is. He must belong to that redheaded father who lives next door to the church." And she was right.

Every man deserves to have a son who looks like his father. On this Father's Day we honor especially those fathers who give their children a good home. That's an identity.

We ought to belong to a good father. But most important, we ought to belong to God. Then our identification is even more certain. "We are the Lord's."

How wonderful to be known as God's child and God's people. We can belong to Him. God is our Heavenly father.

Independence Day

A Joyful Noise

Visual Introduction: A small replica of the Liberty Bell.
Sentence Summary: Let us celebrate and never keep
  quiet about Jesus.
Scripture Text: "Make a joyful noise to the Lord, all the
  lands!" (Ps. 100:1).

Here is a little replica of the original Liberty Bell which
still hangs in Philadelphia, Pennsylvania. Something special happened in that city on the Fourth of July in 1776.
Wise and courageous leaders decided to declare our country's independence from the king of England. So they
wrote what we now call the Declaration of Independence. Then after signing it, they all rushed outside to
shout and rejoice.

Perhaps a few of them had firecrackers, but most people back then made noise with bells. All the church bells
rang that day. But the bell that we best remember ringing
in celebration was that big Liberty Bell on the courthouse
square in Philadelphia.

The Fourth of July is still a happy holiday, not a time to
keep quiet. When we are excited, we want to make a
joyful noise to celebrate. So bring out the bells and celebrate our freedom and independence. No foreign armies
march in our land. That's good news.

When we come to church for worship, we ought to be
just as excited. The psalmist urged us to "Make a joyful
noise to the Lord." This is no time to lean back in your
pew and sleep. Let us celebrate how Jesus Christ came to
earth revealing God's love for us. That's good news worth
shouting about. Ring those bells!

Halloween Season

Remove that Mask!

Visual Introduction: Halloween mask.
Sentence Summary: We can't use a mask to hide from God.
Scripture Text: "Man looks on the outward appearance, but the Lord looks on the heart" (1 Sam. 16:7).

When children finally outgrow their fear of all the Halloween ghosts and goblins, this special season each fall brings fun and games. Children and even adults enjoy dressing up in costumes and hiding their identities behind a mask, such as this one.

How many different masks are being manufactured for our selections? Millions! Some represent cartoon characters, such as Bugs Bunny or Mickey Mouse. Others are formed to look like famous people, such as the president. But most Halloween masks are of the ugly type representing monsters or vicious killers.

Halloween parties are fun because we can keep our identities secret. Of course, we usually don't recognize the other people there either. All evening long people are supposed to guess who is who. What a wonderful game that is.

But some bad people wear masks not for a game but to do wrong. They don't want to be recognized, so they cover their faces. They think a disguise such as this mask will protect them from being caught by the police. That makes the wrongdoer even more bold. He believes he can do anything and always escape because no one knows who he is.

But God is never fooled. You can hide behind the most

clever mask ever devised, but God still knows your identity. You can't hide from God. While people may be fooled by what someone wears, God looks right through the disguise and the mask. The Bible says that "Man looks on the outward appearance, but the Lord looks on the heart." He knows us all too well.

Thanksgiving Season

Promise in a Seed

Visual Introduction: A handful of acorns.

Sentence Summary: Be thankful for seeds which remind us of God's promise for continued life.

Scripture Text: "It is like a grain of mustard seed, which, when sown upon the ground, is the smallest of all the seeds on earth; yet when it is sown it grows up and becomes the greatest of all shrubs, and puts forth large branches, so that the birds of the air can make nests in its shade" (Mark 4:31-32).

Autumn is the season to be thankful for all God's blessings. Today let's be grateful for seeds like this acorn which fell from an oak tree. Every autumn the woods and the meadows ripen with all manner of different seeds like acorns, pine cones, apples, or corn.

The animals and birds feast on these seeds. Of course, we like to eat many seeds like beans, peanuts, corn, and pecans. They make good food which keeps us alive all year long.

But beyond being food, these seeds have a higher purpose. What happens when a tiny acorn falls into the soil? If it is not eaten by deer or birds, then it will sleep until next year. At the proper time in the new season, it begins growing into a giant oak tree. Just imagine. A big tree is inside this acorn.

So inside this seed is the promise of continued life. Whose promise? It is God's promise that the oak trees will not disappear from the face of the earth but will always grow to offer shade for birds and people.

Jesus talked about seeds even smaller than an acorn. In

His country they had mustard trees instead of oaks. The mustard seed was so small that one could hardly see it. Yet it grew into a tree big enough for birds to use for their nests.

In this Thanksgiving season we ought to count our little blessings. Be grateful, not just for big blessings but little blessings which help us continue life.

Christmas Season

The Wrapped Gift

Visual Introduction: Small, gift-wrapped package.
Sentence Summary: God is love.
Scripture Text: "And she gave birth to her first-born son and wrapped him in swaddling cloths" (Luke 2:7). "God is love" (1 John 4:16*b*).

One of the little joys of Christmas is wondering what is inside those packages so brightly wrapped and placed under the Christmas tree. At our home we use strange-sized boxes and always wrap the gifts with heavy paper so no one can see what is inside. That makes it more fun.

Sometimes the best gifts don't come in big, beautiful packages. A big box may look important, but a small package which weighs very little could have something wonderful inside. Perhaps a roll of $100 bills!

When a gift is wrapped, it is just not as obvious. Now I will not unwrap this small gift which I hold right now. It will be best to wait until Christmas.

But let me tell you about the first Christmas gift which God sent to us in an unusual package. It came as a small, living package needing to be immediately wrapped. But not in gift wrapping paper.

A young woman named Mary wrapped the world's most important gift in swaddling cloths. Now do you know what that gift was?

Of course, you know. The first and most important gift of Christmas was given by God. It was the baby Jesus. The woman chosen to be His mother was Mary. She and Joseph wrapped the baby Jesus in long strips of cloth called swaddling cloths. Jesus made the perfect love gift to us.

Christmas Season

The Unopened Gift

Visual Introduction: Large, beautifully wrapped package.
Sentence Summary: The best gift is eternal life from God.
Scripture Text: "But the free gift of God is eternal life in Christ Jesus our Lord" (Rom. 6:23).

Today we have a beautifully wrapped gift. Let's pretend that it is resting under a big Christmas tree ten-feet tall with lots of other gifts. As long as we are pretending, let's agree that every one of those gifts can be for you alone. Would this be a fun dream?

Where would all of these gifts come from? Some would be from your parents and relatives. Others from your friends. Since this is a pleasant daydream, let's make believe that your pastor also includes his gift to you. So all these gifts are for you alone.

Now which is best? You would not know until you open them all, but I can give you a hint. This present which you see (the only one that is not make-believe) represents your very first Christmas gift. It comes from God. Every one of us has been given this free gift.

So what is the gift which God gave to us all? It is the gift of eternal life. God came to earth on that first Christmas to give us a life which begins here on earth and lasts forever in heaven.

We do not deserve this gift. The Bible says that because we have done many bad things called sin, we ought to die. Yet God loves us so much that He offers us a gift instead of death. "But the free gift of God is eternal life in Christ Jesus our Lord."

Now we come to the big question. Will we accept this

gift? Or will we leave this package unopened under the tree?

Some people never accept the best gift of all. They take everything else given to them. They open those packages. Yet they refuse to open the package which has eternal life.

We who believe in God gladly open all of our packages. The gift that we love most, however, is given to us by God. This is eternal life.

Christmas Season

Wants or Needs?

Visual Introduction: A long list of items scrawled on a piece of adding tape.

Sentence Summary: There is a difference between wants and needs.

Scripture Text: "And my God will supply every need of yours according to his riches in glory in Christ Jesus" (Phil. 4:19).

Here is a long list of items some child wrote down while preparing for Christmas. This is something we have all done. We want a new bicycle, a tape player, basketball, doll, wagon, Monopoly game, telephone, television, air rifle, jump rope, boxing gloves, roller skates, and teddy bear. And that's not all. Every time we see something else, we want it. So the list just goes on and on.

But do we always get everything we want? Not at all. We never get everything we want. But so what? We may be disappointed, but we can get along quite well without most of these items. They are not necessary for us to live. Call them "wants." We want them, but we will not die if we do not get them.

On the other hand, some things we really do need like food, a pair of shoes, a house or apartment where we can live, a table and a few chairs, bed, blanket, stove, plates and glasses to eat from—these are all items of genuine need. So we call these "needs."

So there is a big difference between wants and needs. We can get along without the "wants." The things that we need to stay alive are the most important.

The Bible teaches that if we have faith in God, He will

provide those basic things that we need in life. God gives us warm sunshine, hands to work, food to eat, and air to breath. Those are genuine needs provided by God. Listen to this Scripture verse. "My God will supply every need of yours according to his riches in glory in Christ Jesus."

Notice that we are not promised every want. God promises us that He will supply every need. There is a big difference between those two words.

And remember that God gives to us from His riches. He is not poor. He has enough to give and give and yet never be poor. Every need (not want) will be supplied to us according to His riches in glory in Christ.

Christmas Season

The Christmas Crowd

Visual Introduction: Empty sack.
Sentence Summary: Make room for Jesus.
Scripture Text: "And she gave birth to her first-born son and wrapped him in swaddling cloths, and laid him in a manger, because there was no place for him in the inn" (Luke 2:7).

Christmas is the season for crowds. People gather to shop at stores, to enjoy parties with friends, or to worship at church. Crowds gather everywhere. But it was also crowded that first Christmas. Remember how the city of Bethlehem was crowded because Caesar Augustus had ordered a worldwide tax. To make sure everyone was properly counted, every citizen had to return to the main city of his ancestors. That is why Joseph and Mary went to Bethlehem.

By the time they arrived, everyone else had already taken the few available rooms. There was no room left at the inn. So Jesus was born in the only place available—a stable among the animals. But even the stable became crowded later that night.

Today we will demonstrate how crowded that stable around the manger must have been. I was going to bring a miniature manger scene with me, but the pieces were just too many. That's why this sack is empty. Perhaps you can help me remember the characters around the original manger.

Let's begin with the animals. Surely some lovable lambs were present. Two or three of you can stand now to represent the lambs. Next the cows. And also a couple of donkeys. Perhaps some goats were present. As I point to you, you may represent one of these animals.

Next comes the big people. We need a Mary and a Joseph. Then three or four can become shepherds. Don't forget the Wise Men. Three or four of you can also stand for camels which brought the Wise Men.

Now that is quite a crowd. I believe we have everyone —unless you want to include the innkeeper and his wife. They provided the stable.

(Note: At this point some astute little observer will certainly recognize your obvious omission. You have not chosen anyone to represent the baby Jesus. In the midst of a crowd, we have forgotten Jesus! Now you can conclude with this theme of making room for Jesus.)

Part II
Sermons for Special Sundays

Senior Adult Day
Revival
Stewardship Sunday
Homecoming
Scout Sunday
Youth Sunday

Senior Adult Day

Alive at Eighty-Five!

Visual Introduction: A walking cane.
Sentence Summary: People can be both old and strong.
Scripture Text: "Look at me! I am eighty-five years old and am just as strong today as I was when Moses sent me out. I am still strong enough for war or anything else" (Josh. 14:10-11, GNB).

Here is a walking cane for people who are old. Anyone old must be weak and in need of a good walking cane. Right? Wrong!

Today is Senior Adult Day in our church. Look around and you see people with gray hair, wrinkles on their faces, and perhaps a few walking canes. These people may seem old and weak to you. But don't be fooled. Being old does not mean the same as being weak. Let me tell you the story of Caleb, a man who lived many years but never seemed to get old. He lived a long time because he obeyed God. He was one of the most faithful helpers for Moses.

When God's people arrived in the Promised Land, Caleb spoke to the leader who followed Moses. His name was Joshua. Caleb reminded Joshua of the promise that Moses made to Caleb forty-five years earlier. Moses had promised that if Caleb remained faithful and obeyed God, then Caleb would receive some special hill country where giants lived. But Caleb was not afraid of giants. He wanted his land and was willing to fight the giants.

But Caleb was no longer a young man. Perhaps some people would think he was too old to fight for what Moses had promised him. Yet listen to how Caleb described himself: "Look at me! I am eighty-five years old and just as strong today as I was when Moses sent me out. I am still strong enough for war or for anything else."

That's the spirit. Just because people live to be eighty-five years old, don't call them old! Call them eighty-five years young. Very few people ever need this cane. Today we honor senior adults by understanding how they can live many years and still be strong.

Revival

Harvest Colors

Visual Introduction: A pumpkin.
Sentence Summary: This is now the season of spiritual harvest to bring people to God.
Scripture Text: "Do you not say, 'There are yet four months, then comes the harvest'? I tell you, lift up your eyes, and see how the fields are already white for harvest" (John 4:35).

Revival time is harvest time. What is your favorite color of harvest? The farmer knew when this pumpkin was ready to pick because pumpkins turn bright orange at harvest time. He did not pick the pumpkin in August when it was green, but he waited until September when the color was right.

A tomato turns red. Wheat, oats, and barley turn a kind of golden brown. Leaves on an oak tree mature into a mixture of many colors warning us that it is harvesttime with acorns falling to the ground. Every fruit and vegetable has a proper time for harvest.

Why is it so important to look for the right colors during harvest? If we wait too long and ignore the harvest, then the fruits and vegetables lose their freshness. Heavy rain or hail might destroy the crop. So when the harvest is ready, we must be ready.

Jesus once looked across fields and saw a crop in urgent need of harvesting. But this was not the ordinary harvest of grain or fruit. Jesus saw people dressed in the traditional white robes which people wore in that time. That field looked white. Although four months remained before the fall harvest of grain, Jesus told his disciples to look up and see how the fields of people were already white for harvest. It was time to bring those people into God's kingdom. They must be told about Jesus.

We wonder if Jesus had ever seen a cotton field with the cotton bolls swelled open and ready to pick. Those cotton fields are truly white for harvest. In the same way, in any crowd of people today are many individuals ready and waiting for us to bring them into God's church. Now is the time! Revival is harvesttime.

Stewardship Sunday

Empty-Handed

Visual Introduction: An empty suitcase.

Sentence Summary: Things of this world ought not become too important to us since we cannot take them with us to heaven.

Scripture Text: "For we brought nothing into the world, and we cannot take anything out of the world" (1 Tim. 6:7).

The first thing we usually do with planning a long trip is to drag a suitcase out of the closet. Then we pack it with all the necessary things we need during that trip away from home. Can you suggest some important things that we would need to pack in this suitcase if we were going to spend a wonderful week at church camp?

Yes, we would need a Bible, toothpaste, clean underwear, and extra shoes. Don't forget raisins or some other good snacks for late at night. Finally, we ought to pack some paper and envelopes for writing home. Those are all good things to have with us while we are gone.

But what if our trip is to be out of this world? What will we need to take with us to heaven? *Nothing.* Absolutely nothing. We will not have any needs in heaven. God will provide everything that we could ever want when we get to heaven.

Perhaps you want to take along your favorite baseball bat or your favorite doll. Maybe you cannot bear to think about leaving behind certain books, photographs, and other treasures. But there is no way to take those treasures. The Bible tells us firmly: "For we brought nothing into the world, and we cannot take anything out of the world" (1 Tim. 6:7).

Empty-handed. That's how we came into this world, and that is how we leave. So we ought not become too attached to things in this world. That fact ought to help us become more generous here on earth. We should give generously unto God because we can't keep it anyway. In heaven we will have everything we need. Best of all, we will be with Jesus!

Stewardship Sunday

Cooperation

Visual Introduction: Construction blueprints or a list of supplies needed for building a church building.

Sentence Summary: With everyone's help God's people can do anything.

Scripture Text: "The people bring much more than enough for doing the work which the Lord has commanded us to do" (Ex. 36:5).

Today we meet in this church building which you children did not build. Your parents and grandparents may have helped earlier, but the great task is already complete. But how would we build this house of God?

We would need lumber, bricks, nails, windows, doors, and roofing material. When we got it all built, then we would still need chairs, tables, pews, musical instruments, books, and lots of other things. They all cost money.

In every crowd are a few people who will be afraid to start work. They say, "This is a job too big for the few of us. We ought to wait. Let's delay until we have more people."

But others say, "We can trust God to help us. If we all give and work hard, then we can complete this building."

That is what happened a long time ago when God's people wanted to build the first place of worship. They called it a tabernacle. Everyone agreed to bring something valuable like gold, silver, or building materials like wood and stone. No one made them do this. They gave from willing hearts.

Some probably said: "It can never be done!" But most

of the people did not listen to those discouraging words. They just kept bringing gifts to build God's house.

Finally one day the workmen told Moses: "The people bring much more than enough for doing the work which the Lord has commanded us to do." So Moses told them to stop. They had enough to build the tabernacle.

What a wonderful spirit of cooperation. God's people can do anything together. But they must keep on working even after the church house is built. Later the building needs painting and repairs. Money is needed for electricity and water.

So if you come along too late to help build this church house, then be happy. You can still give your gifts to keep it open. Wouldn't it be wonderful for all the people today to give so much that the pastor would need to say: "The people bring more than enough"?

Stewardship Sunday

How to Give Gladly

Visual Introduction: A pair of boxing gloves and an offer-
  ing plate.
Sentence Summary: God loves us to give in a glad spirit.
Scripture Text: "Each one should give, then, as he has
  decided, not with regret or out of a sense of duty; for
  God loves the one who gives gladly" (2 Cor. 9:7, GNB).

Today we have an offering plate which looks very familiar in church. It belongs in church. But what are these
boxing gloves doing here today? When we come to
church, we expect the offering plate will be passed. People who love God just want to give to God. They are
generous and happy in giving.

Boxing gloves are for people who wish to fight. When
the big boys at school get mad at one another and threat-
en to fight, the coach may say: "All right boys, put on the
boxing gloves. If you want to fight, then go ahead and
fight."

Some people do not like to give. They are very stingy.
When the offering plate appears or the preacher begins
talking about money, they act as if they are angry. Perhaps the only thing they want to give is a punch in the
nose to the usher who passes the offering plate by them.

Of course, we are only joking. Boxing gloves have no
place in church. The pastor does not use boxing gloves on
his members who may not wish to give. Neither can
church members use boxing gloves to beat up the ushers
or the pastor.

The Bible says that each one of us must decide how
much he will give to God. This is our decision to make. No

one forces us to donate. And when we give, we do so gladly. We ought not give in an angry spirit. God wants us to give gladly. We should be happy to give without any regrets or sorrow.

Then what happens? God loves everyone who gives gladly. He loves to see us happy, and we are really happy when giving freely to God.

Homecoming

Always Home

Visual Introduction: A turtle.
Sentence Summary: Homecoming is a time to tell what the Lord has done for us.
Scripture Text: "Go home to your friends, and tell them how much the Lord has done for you, and how he has had mercy on you" (Mark 5:19).

The turtle reminds us of an ancient riddle. "What creature always travels but never leaves home?" The answer is easy. We see turtles crawling around every place. They never stay in one spot. As long as they live, they keep on the move.

Look at this turtle. Even now he wants to crawl away. He isn't worried about where he will stay. No matter where he goes, he always takes his house with him. His shell is like a travel camper or a cozy tent. Whenever he gets tired and wants to rest, his house is right there for safety and comfort. Home sweet home!

Today we welcome back many who have traveled and now live someplace else. This is homecoming for them. They have returned to the annual event to share good memories and to renew ties with us who remain here in their church home. We've kept the home fires burning for them.

Homecoming is a happy occasion. But those who have left to live elsewhere need not wait for an official event like homecoming to return. We will rejoice with anyone who comes back at any time of the year.

Jesus once healed a man who had been crazy. He had forsaken his family and friends and lived as a wild man in a graveyard. No one could keep him calm. Whenever he was caught and his hands tied with chains, he broke them and fled in a fit of rage.

But Jesus calmed that wild man into a gentle, loving soul. Everyone was amazed. The restored man wanted to go with Jesus, but our Lord gave him orders. "Go home to your friends, and tell them how much the Lord has done for you, and how he has had mercy on you."

That must have been a happy homecoming. The people at home needed him, and he needed them. From then on he would never run away. He would always be at home.

Scout Sunday

Be Prepared

Visual Introduction: Fire-starting materials
Sentence Summary: Plan now to be prepared for God.
Scripture Text: "Prepare your hearts unto the Lord, and serve him only" (1 Sam. 7:3, KJV).

Would you like to go camping with a group of boy scouts? That sounds fun. Boy scouts know how to cook good food over a campfire. But first they need a fire, so here are some materials which can be used to start the fire. Dry tender. Bits of leaves. A piece of flint to produce a spark. And presto! A fire soon blazes hot.

The motto for boy scouts is: "Be prepared." These fire-starting materials help them be prepared to start that fire. As those boys grow in the scout traditions, they learn about this ancient method of starting a fire without matches. These dry materials will start burning with only a spark. Then the scouts pile on twigs and leaves and soon they have a roaring campfire ready to cook their food.

Now wouldn't it be foolish for a troop of boy scouts to arrive in the woods and begin asking one another, "Who is going to start the fire?" Or, "How can we build a fire?" You would never hear boy scouts talking like that.

Just as boy scouts prepare themselves for camping and building fires, so we must prepare ourselves to serve God. Long ago a wise man named Samuel offered some good advice to the people of his nation. He told them to "Prepare your hearts unto the Lord, and serve him only."

Belonging to God is no casual matter. We ought to gather every week, preparing our hearts for the Lord. Like scouts who study and practice lessons such as building a fire, so we should work hard at prayer and Bible study.

Youth Sunday

The Boy Who Hurt the Man

Visual Introduction: A crutch.
Sentence Summary: Take care of your body.
Scripture Text: "Do you not know that your body is a temple of the Holy Spirit within you, which you have from God? You are not your own; you are bought with a price. So glorify God in your body" (1 Cor. 6:19-20).

How can a crutch be associated with Youth Sunday? You children don't seem to need a crutch. And certainly our youth whom we honor today don't want to be slowed down long enough to need one. But this crutch reminds me of an old man who saw some boys riding their bicycles in a dangerous manner. They were so careless playing in the street that he offered to tell them the story of his crutch.

He explained how long ago he used to be good at riding bicycles. No one could ride faster or turn a sharper circle in the middle of busy traffic than he could.

"Then one day a boy just your age did this to me. His carelessness caused an accident which kept me from ever riding my bicycle again. I have walked on crutches the rest of my life."

The children were shocked. "That mean boy ought to be punished," they said.

"He was," replied the old man. "And even though that boy has now grown into an old man, he is still being punished today."

"Serves him right," they said. "But who was that mean boy?" they asked.

"The boy who did that to me is the same boy I used to be."

Now the children were confused. So the old man continued: "I was acting then just as you children are acting now. I failed to understand that my body does not belong to me. It belongs to God, so I ought to take good care of it. Because of my carelessness, I became handicapped as a boy. I'm a man now but still must use a crutch to walk. The boy that I was then hurt the man that I am now."

And that's the story of the boy who hurt the man. The Bible teaches us that we don't belong to ourselves. In 1 Corinthians 6:19-20 we find that our bodies should be temples where God lives. God owns us. So be careful. Don't hurt the body of the person God wants you to become when you grow up.

Part III
Easy Interviews

Football Player's Interview

Wear Your Armor!

Visual Introduction: A football player in full gear.

Sentence Summary: As a football player needs proper equipment to keep him safe, so Christians need spiritual armor to fight the devil.

Scripture Text: "Put on all the armor that God gives you, so that you will be able to stand against the Devil's evil tricks" (Eph. 6:11, GNB).

Today we can easily recognize this person as a football player. Will you children meet Mr. _____ who plays for the _____ team. Mr. _____, could you explain the purpose of your uniform and gear which you have worn? Let's begin with your helmet.

Guest: "Pastor, the most important football gear I wear is this helmet which protects my head from hard blows. The head is a fragile part of a tough player's body.

I also wear protective pads over my elbows and knees to prevent scratches. The thick pads on my shoulders are much like armor. They make me look much bigger and also cushion my shoulder bones which could break.

Notice that the pants are tight, so my opponents cannot easily grab hold of me while I am running. Then, finally, I am wearing shoes with cleats on the bottom, so I won't slip and fall down.

Pastor: Thank you for explaining how the uniform you wear is like a protective armor to keep you safe. We Christians are familiar with armor because Paul warned the Ephesian Christians about how sneaky is our opponent, the devil. Rather than playing games, he is trying to hurt us.

This is spiritual war. We need protection like armor. Ephesians 6:11 tells us to "Put on all the armor that God gives you, so that you will be able to stand against the Devil's evil tricks."

What type of armor? It must be spiritual armor in this spiritual war. Truth and faith are required. Salvation is necessary. Listen as we read further from Ephesians 6:14-17: "So stand ready, with truth as a belt tight around your waist, with righteousness as your breastplate, and as your shoes the readiness to announce the Good News of peace. At all times carry faith as a shield; for with it you will be able to put out all the burning arrows shot by the Evil One. And accept salvation as a helmet, and the word of God as the sword which the Spirit gives you" (GNB).

A Fisherman's Interview

The Good and the Bad

Visual Introduction: Fisherman holding a fish net.

Sentence Summary: People, like fish, are either good or bad.

Scripture Text: "Again, the kingdom of heaven is like a net which was thrown into the sea and gathered fish of every kind; when it was full, men drew it ashore and sat down and sorted the good into vessels but threw away the bad. So it will be at the close of the age. The angels will come out and separate the evil from among the righteous, and throw them into the furnace of fire; there men will weep and gnash their teeth" (Matt. 13: 47-50).

Our guest today is a fisherman. He has a hat with hooks plus a basket for the fish he catches. But why does he not have a fishing pole? Let's ask Mr. _____ why he is carrying a net instead of a pole?

Guest: Pastor, a fishing pole is good for catching fish one at a time. But wouldn't it be quicker to catch many fish at the same time with a net?

This net reminds us how people used to fish for food in Bible times. Today's modern fishermen have bigger ships and catch more fish, but they still use the same type net in the oceans.

After the catch comes the crucial choice. Which fish are good to keep, and which are bad? Those with tough skins, bad tasting meat, or too many bones aren't worth keeping for food. They are thrown away or used for products like fertilizer. But they are basically useless for food.

Is the fish good or bad? It must be one or the other. The

fisherman either keeps it or throws it away. There is no middle ground.

Pastor: That is a good lesson for us today. Jesus taught us that, like the fish in Jesus' story, people are either good or bad. But at least we have a choice. We choose to be good, or we choose to be bad. Without Jesus as Savior we are as worthless as bad fish. But when we allow Jesus into our hearts, then we become very valuable.

At the end of the world, Jesus is coming back with His angels to judge which people are good and which are bad. We will all be swept up into His net like a fisherman catches fish. Those who refused to cooperate with God will be judged as "bad." He will throw them into a furnace that burns forever.

But those who belong to Jesus need not fear. He will gather them unto Himself and keep them forever.

Interview with a Physician

The Doctor Needs a Doctor

Visual Introduction: A physician with stethoscope
Sentence Summary: God made us all as sinners.
Scripture Text: "All have sinned and fall short of the glory of God" (Rom. 3:23).

Today we have another guest. This is Dr. _____ who lives in our community. He may already be the doctor for your family.

Doctor, we are glad to have you. And I am glad to know you. The children may not realize it, but a pastor sometimes needs a doctor. When I am cut, I bleed just like anyone else. If I become sick, you might need to help me. What do you say to that?

Guest: Well, pastor, everyone ought to know that you are human. When you get sick, you need a doctor just like everyone else. But let me be even more honest with the children.

Although I am a doctor who helps other people get well, I also need a doctor. When I am cut, I bleed just like the pastor and you children bleed. After all, God made us all alike.

So I need a doctor, too. But your pastor and I share yet another need with you children. We need a Savior like Jesus. God says we all have the same terrible problem. We are all sinners. Instead of being strong and doing good deeds all the time, we get angry or say bad things. Those are sins. And all it takes is just one sin for each of us to be a sinner. That's the worst kind of sickness—spiritual sickness caused by sin. Pastor, can you tell them more?

Pastor: Just as a sick person must admit to being sick and

then ask a doctor for help, so we must admit to being a sinner before God can help us. So we all agree with Romans 3:23: "All have sinned and fall short of the glory of God."

Interview with a Blind Person

The Blind See

Visual Introduction: A blind person with braille Bible or
  hymn book.
Sentence Summary: God helps us see.
Scripture Truth: "One thing I know, that though I was
  blind, now I see" (John 9:25*b*).

Today we have a guest who has brought an interesting
book to demonstrate. This person's name is _____. Although she is blind, she can do something none of you can
do. She can read in the dark! "Mrs. _____, can you explain that?

Guest: Pastor, my eyes cannot see the beauties of God's
earth, so you are correct to say that I am blind. But not
when it comes to reading beautiful truths from the Bible.
I use soft fingertips God gave me to read this special Book.
I read by feeling special bumps on the pages of this Bible
which is printed for blind people. These raised dots or
bumps spell words to me in the same way that people read
black ink on white paper.

It was not easy at first. But because I wanted to see, I
learned to read these bumps by attending a special school
which teaches this system. These bumps were designed
by a man named Mr. Braille. That is why we call it the
braille system of reading.

Pastor: You remind me of a blind man in the Bible. God
helped him to see by healing his eyes. So he said, "One
thing I know, that though I was blind, now I see." He was
very happy to see wonderful things in God's world after
he had been blind. And now you can see, too. The best
sight of all is whenever anyone can see God's Word.

Interview with a Policeman

Submission

Interest Object: A policeman in uniform.
Main Truth: We must learn to submit ourselves to authority.
Scripture Text: "Everyone must submit himself to the governing authorities, for there is no authority except that which God has established. The authorities that exist have been established by God" (Rom. 13:1, NIV).

You may have never met our guest today, but you will recognize the uniform. His name is _____. Officer, you have come today to talk about submission. What does it mean to submit or be under submission?

Guest: To submit means to obey. People obey a policeman or submit to laws and rules. They agree to drive only on the right-hand side of a road. Imagine the danger if everyone decided to drive right down the middle! When everyone submits to the rules, then we have a good idea of which side the other car takes.

Rules and laws help keep us safe. Aren't you glad that we have laws making it wrong for others to take away our money? That's stealing, and it is wrong. We policemen catch law-breakers and put them in jail for stealing. Or we issue traffic tickets to those who drive too fast. In that way we help keep you safe.

So the laws protect us. But only if everyone agrees to obey the laws. We must submit to laws and to those who enforce them.

I believe the Bible teaches us to submit to the governing authorities. Pastor, could you find that for us in the Bible?

Pastor: Yes, the Bible says that we must submit ourselves to people like policemen because God has given that authority to them. It is God's plan for policemen to protect us and keep our country safe. Let's read Romans 13:1: "Everyone must submit himself to the governing authorities, for there is no authority except that which God has established. The authorities that exist have been established by God" (NIV).

Interview With A Cook

Let Us Rise

Visual Introduction: Cook holding a cup of warm water with yeast.

Sentence Summary: God is at work among us.

Scripture Text: "Jesus told them still another parable: 'The Kingdom of heaven is like yeast. A woman takes some yeast and mixes it with a bushel of flour until the whole batch of dough rises'" (Matt. 13:33, GNB).

This nice lady (or gentleman) in an apron may be familiar to you. She cooks at our church (or school) and has brought something which smells good in a cup. Her name is _____. Could you tell us, Mrs. _____, what smells so good?

Guest: Earlier today I put in this cup some warm water and a small amount of yeast. I also added just a little flour and sugar so the yeast could begin growing. What we now smell is the flavor of homemade bread. Ah, it smells so good because the yeast is at work doing what it is supposed to do.

As the yeast multiplies and grows, it makes small air bubbles which causes the flour to swell up bigger. We say that the bread is rising. The difference between a cracker and a piece of bread is just a little bit of simple yeast. Crackers have no yeast to make them swell or rise into "light bread."

Didn't Jesus talk about yeast, Pastor?

Pastor: Yes, in the Bible yeast is often described as leaven. A little bit of it working hard can change a lot of dough. Listen to this verse from a modern version where Jesus talks about yeast which reminds Him of the kingdom of heaven here on earth. "The kingdom of heaven is like yeast. A woman takes some yeast and mixes it with a bushel of flour until the whole batch of dough rises" (GNB).

What does Jesus mean? He looks at this old world and sees His people doing what God wants them to do. Although few in number, they work like leaven because God is at work in their hearts. Not everyone works for God. Indeed, it seems that most people do nothing for God. But the people busy for God can do enough to change the whole world just as a little yeast can change a whole bushel of flour into bread.

We are supposed to be like that. When we who love Jesus work for Him, we can change the entire world.

Part IV
All-Purpose Occasions

Children's sermons in this section can be used for all-purpose occasions including regular worship, Vacation Bible School, children's church sessions, etc.

The Foreigner
The Magic Vest
Love Lights
Be Firm
Travelers to Heaven
Living Water
Who's Who?
Light for a Dark World
Resist
The Protector
In Time of Trouble
Be Positive
A Better Pump
Be a Friend
Believe in Things Not Seen
Finding God
No Losers with the Lord

The Foreigner

Visual Introduction: Bible in Spanish.

Sentence Summary: To understand God and His Bible we must belong to Him.

Scripture Text: "Whoever does not have the Spirit cannot receive the gifts that come from God's Spirit. Such a person really does not understand them; they are nonsense to him" (1 Cor. 2:14, GNB).

Some of you are old enough now to read books at school, newspapers at home, and even the Bible in church. I am going to ask one of you older children to read a few verses from this Bible. The person I pick will read to all of us.

Wait a minute. We seem to have some difficulty here because our volunteer reader has not begun to read. Do you see how he looks at the Bible with a strange expression? He sees words written with our alphabet. But they do not make sense to him.

By now some of you have guessed what is wrong. This Bible is not written in English but rather in a foreign language. It is written in Spanish. To read this Bible you must be able to speak and read Spanish. To us who do not speak Spanish, that language is a foreign tongue. Therefore, we cannot understand this Bible until we understand the language.

Some people know English but still cannot understand the Bible. The problem is very similar. They are foreigners to God. Because they do not accept God, they cannot understand what this Bible really means.

Oh, those who do not belong to God can recognize the words but not the true and full meaning. Some of these verses sound as strange to them as a foreign tongue. But if they will let Jesus come into their hearts and change them into a new person, then God will help them understand. They receive the gift of understanding God's Word.

In 1 Corinthians 2 Paul explained how people who are foreigners to God just cannot understand God's truths. "Whoever does not have the Spirit cannot receive the gifts that come from God's Spirit. Such a person really does not understand them; they are nonsense to him" (GNB).

The Magic Vest

Visual Introduction: A colorful vest.
Sentence Summary: Don't be selfish.
Scripture Text: "Don't think only of yourself. Try to think of the other fellow, too, and what is best for him" (1 Cor. 10:24, TLB).

Today I'm wearing a colorful vest. Let's pretend that this vest is magic. An angel brings it to me, explaining that when I wear it, then I can help others have whatever they need.

For example, I may see someone who is very hungry. Then I can wish for that person to have food. The angel will deliver whatever I ask to that person. That will be wonderful!

Will you grant my every wish? "Yes," the angel replies. "But be careful. Don't be selfish and use the magic power of the vest for yourself. Save it for others."

What if I use some of the magic power to make an ice cream cone just for me? The wish will come true, but the vest will become tighter and squeeze me!

I accept the vest on those terms, promising not to be selfish. I must help others instead of using the power for myself.

So the first day I wear the vest and meet a family with no food. I feel sorry for them and say, "I wish for them a delicious hot meal." Presto! It works. They have lots of food. That makes me very happy.

But I start thinking. I wish I had a big piece of pie like they have. Presto! A piece of pie appears for me. While eating I notice that the vest became tighter, however. I must be careful to make no more selfish wishes.

But it happens again and again. I think of so many things I want. Instead of trying to help others with my new power, I wind up wishing for things like pretty clothes or a new car. I get them each time, but also the vest becomes tighter.

You can guess the rest of this story, can't you? Finally one day, my selfishness causes me to be squeezed to death.

Now that is just a make-believe story, but in some ways it is true. Most of us are so selfish. We always think of ourselves instead of the other person. That attitude causes us much pain.

The Bible tells us to think what is best for others. Rather than satisfy our own desires, we should do good things for others. They will be blessed. We will be happy.

"Don't think only of yourself. Try to think of the other fellow, too, and what is best for him."

Love Lights

Visual Introduction: Reflector light.
Sentence Summary: Let God's love light shine in you.
Scripture Text: "We love, because he first loved us" (1 John 4:19).

Here is a light which can never shine by itself. That is the bad news. But this little light is not sad because it cannot shine with its own light. It does something other lights can't do. It can shine in total darkness.

We call this a reflector light. A reflector is much like a mirror. It reflects whatever light comes to it. It can be placed on a mailbox beside the road or on a gate across the road so people will not run over the mailbox or into the gate when driving at night. If this place were totally dark right now, someone could shine a light from far away. When that light strikes this reflector lamp, it returns every bit of the light back to the source. It shows light because someone first gave it light.

Love is like a light. The love that we feel in our hearts for God shines forth. But that love did not begin within us. We do not create love. We reflect it. The Bible says that "We love, because he first loved us."

The love which we have for God and for others came first of all from God. So we ought to be like a reflector light which takes that light and bounces it back. That way others can see God's love in us.

Be Firm

Visual Introduction: Picture of a camel.
Sentence Summary: Don't allow little sins into your heart because they can take over your whole life.
Scripture Text: "Avoid every kind of evil" (1 Thess. 5:22, NIV).

An old story from the Arab world tells about a traveler asleep one night in his cozy tent. Outside the cold desert winds were keeping his camel awake, so the animal barely stuck his nose through the tent door.

"Hey, camel, what are you doing?" the man inside yelled.

"Oh, master, it is so cold out here that my nose is freezing. Surely it wouldn't hurt anything for my nose barely to remain inside your tent."

That sounded reasonable enough, so the man agreed. Then he went back to sleep, but it wasn't long when he felt the warm smelly breath of a camel. "Say, I didn't tell you to stick you full head in here. Only your nose."

The camel pleaded for mercy and promised that only his nose and head would remain in the tent. The man could go back to sleep. Everything would be all right. So the man again agreed to that reasonable request. After all, there wasn't much difference between a nose and a head.

Well, you can guess the rest of this story. Next the camel wanted only his front shoulder inside. And then more and more. Finally the traveler wound up outside in the cold covered with sand. Somehow he had been crowded out of his own tent by the camel who was now sleeping comfortably inside. It started with the harmless nose of a camel, but look what it led to.

Sin is like that. You may be tempted to do something that doesn't sound very bad. It is just a little sin. The devil whispers to you, "This won't matter much. Go ahead and do it."

Be careful! The camel has just stuck his nose in your tent. You can be sure that if you allow a little sin into your life, it will start growing, and soon it will get worse. It may take over your whole life.

The Bible warns us about sin and evil. "Avoid every kind of evil" (NIV).

Travelers to Heaven

Visual Introduction: A traveler's passport.
Sentence Summary: The best trip of all is our journey to heaven.
Scripture Text: "By faith he sojourned in the land of promise, as in a foreign land, living in tents with Isaac and Jacob, heirs with him of the same promise" (Heb. 11:9).

Here is my passport which I use when traveling in foreign lands. If you wish to travel with me, you cannot use my passport. You must get one for yourself with your own picture inside. The authorities will examine it carefully before allowing you to enter their country.

What kind of questions will they ask when you travel in a strange land? No matter where you go, the people in charge at the border will examine your passport and then always ask the same questions.

The first question they ask is, "Where were you born?" Your answer reveals your nationality. If you were born in Canada, then you are a Canadian. Canada is your country.

We would not want to confuse those people, but we Christians can give a different answer to that question. We who belong to Jesus Christ can say, "I was born the second time in Jesus Christ during a moment of worship in such and such place. Therefore, I belong to God's kingdom."

The second question is, "Where are you going?" They want to know your destination. Well, we Christians certainly know where we are going. We are travelers to heaven. No matter where we live or where we visit, we know that life is only temporary here on earth. Every country to us is like a foreign land because we are on our way to heaven.

The final question asked by the customs inspector is, "What are you taking with you?" He wants to know if we have any tobacco, alcohol, drugs, or merchandise bought elsewhere. These purchases may be illegal in some countries. Or we may owe tax on these items.

But when traveling to heaven, we won't be taking anything from earth. We go empty handed. So we can truthfully say, "I'm taking nothing with me because my Father in heaven has everything already prepared for me which I'll need there."

So traveling to a foreign land does involve questions. But we believers in Jesus Christ have good answers. The best trip of all is that journey to heaven.

Living Water

Visual Introduction: Sponge
Sentence Summary: Jesus is like water which satisfies a thirsty soul.
Scripture Text: "But whoever drinks of the water that I shall give him will never thirst" (John 4:14).

Here is something dry, hard, flat, and lifeless. In this present condition it is also useless. What is it? You are right. This is a sponge.

Now what does a sponge need to become useful? Again you know the answer to that question. To become soft and fluffy a sponge needs water.

This sponge was born in water on the deep bottom of the ocean. Even with holes in it, it can still hold water. When kept wet, it helps us in washing cars. A sponge can be used in cleaning the refrigerator door or countertop. So as long as we have water, we have a useful sponge. The more water, the better.

It seems that a sponge never has enough water. It is always searching for more water to keep itself clean and useful. But if it dries out, it becomes useless.

What does the Bible say about sponges? Nothing. But the Bible tells us much about Jesus who is often compared to water. So let's talk about water.

Jesus satisfies a deep thirst within us. Like a sponge, we crave something similar to water. We need the water of eternal life.

Our Lord promised to satisfy our deepest need, a spiritual thirst we've had ever since birth. When we accept Jesus as our Savior, we are finally satisfied for this need of the spirit. As Jesus said, "But whoever drinks of the water that I shall give him will never thirst" (John 4:14).

Who's Who?

Visual Introduction: Church bulletin with names of leaders.

Sentence Summary: Each of us has many special tasks to do in church.

Scripture Text: "So we are to use our different gifts in accordance with the grace that God has given us. If our gift is to preach God's message, we should do it according to the faith that we have; if it is to serve, we should serve; if it is to teach, we should teach; if it is to encourage others, we should do so" (Rom. 12:6-8, GNB).

Somewhere on nearly every church bulletin for Sunday worship you will find a list of names. In many churches the names of the pastor and staff are listed. Other churches list their leaders or officers. They want us to know who is who.

The Bible teaches in Romans 12 that every Christian has a different talent or gift which he or she can use in church. Don't be confused by the word *gifts.* The word means talents or abilities to do certain jobs in church. For example, the pastor must be able to stand behind the pulpit and preach. The one who plays a piano must study hard and prepare to make beautiful music which helps God's people sing. Those are abilities or spiritual gifts.

(Now the Scripture can be read at this point.)

Someone must lead the music. Others teach in the Bible classes. Still others love the babies in the church nursery. So everyone has a job to do in the church.

Perhaps the bulletin cannot always list every worker in church. But at least it can remind us by the names listed, that every task in the church needs a special person gifted with an ability to accomplish that task.

Light for a Dark World

Visual Introduction: A burning candle.
Sentence Summary: Jesus is light for our dark world.
Scripture Text: "Again Jesus spoke to them, saying, 'I am the light of the world; he who follows me will not walk in darkness, but will have the light of life' " (John 8:12).

The object we see here is certainly one of the most familiar in all the world. No matter what country, from the cold North Pole to the hot jungle regions, everyone uses candles.

While Jesus was growing up, all children knew about light from clay lamps. Later candles were invented. And even today in our modern space age, we still recognize candles. They are an old-fashioned, never-fail source of light ready for any emergency. If the electricity quits and plunges us into darkness, we need not stumble around for long. Bring out the candles! We will have light.

When Jesus wanted to introduce Himself in a way everyone could understand, He used light as an illustration. What a bright idea! Listen to His own words found in John

8:12. "I am the light of the world; he who follows me will not walk in darkness, but will have the light of life."

Without Jesus we are lost in a spiritual darkness. We do not know right from wrong. We cannot see to help others. Neither can we see the way to help ourselves.

So Jesus became a light to show us God. If we follow the light of Jesus, we will not walk in darkness. Our paths can be well lit. Our lives can be filled with light.

The Protector

Visual Introduction: Lovable-looking stuffed dog.
Sentence Summary: The God who is within us is greater than the devil or anyone else who is in the world.
Scripture Text: "For he who is in you is greater than he who is in the world" (1 John 4:4).

Recently I was jogging at night and felt like going a little farther than usual. Normally I stay on the same path because all the dogs know me and don't even bark when I run past their homes. While going down a different road, however, a big white dog suddenly surprised me. He barked and growled fiercely.

Did I try to run harder and get away? No, I stopped right in my tracks, turned, and looked that old dog right in the eyes. "Get!"

Well, that shocked the dog. He stopped in his tracks and looked me over very carefully. I believe he was thinking, *Well, I wasn't going to bite you anyway. But if you are going to come down my street, just be careful. I'm not the only tough dog around here. Perhaps I could be your friend, and you could be a master for me. I'll just trot along and protect you from all the other mean dogs in this neighborhood.*

And that's just what he did. Every time another dog came challenging me, he would growl at his friends and tell them to leave this stranger alone. He became my protector.

Because I jog close to his neighborhood nearly every night, he often waits for me two or three blocks away from his home. He lets me know that when I want to come along his way, he will protect me. He often jogs with me a couple of miles before going back home. We have become good friends.

The Bible teaches us that God is our Protector. But not just along beside us. When we invite Him inside our lives, He comes to stay. Jesus wants us to know that we will never be alone. He is greater than anyone else in this world, so we need not be afraid. "For he who is in you is greater than he who is in the world."

In Time of Trouble

Visual Introduction: A thin crosscut of a tree showing growth rings.
Sentence Summary: Tough times pass, so be patient.
Scripture Text: "Be patient in tribulation" (Rom. 12:12*b*).

Have you ever seen the living history of a tree? This piece of wood came from a tree many years old. If you count all of these rings, you learn the exact age of this tree. That is because the tree has a separate growth ring for every year it lives.

Notice that not all the growth rings are equal. Some years this tree grew very well. Those were good years with lots of rain and sunshine.

Other years were tough for this tree. Perhaps it did not rain much for several years in a row. Scientists studying the rings of these trees can accurately describe weather patterns for years long past.

For example, the last ring represents the year the tree was cut. Each ring counts backward in time. So the tree can tell the story of its good times and bad times. This record is like a personal diary.

Yes, this tree saw some terrible times. Just like we people sometimes see. We call bad times by a variety of names, like trouble or tribulation. The Bible warns us that tribulations come to every person. But when things don't go easy, do we quit living? Do we simply give up?

Of course not. We know that life gets better. We must be patient in times of tribulation. Tough times never last. As you can see from these tree rings, tomorrow can be better. When things looked real bad, then everything would change. The weather would improve, and the tree could resume happy growth.

The tree is one of God's most patient creations. Just because it may not have much water one year, it does not give up and die. It patiently waits for better times. And God expects us to do the same. "Be patient in tribulation."

Be Positive

Visual Introduction: Small spot or smudge on poster board.
Sentence Summary: Think and do good things.
Scripture Text: "Hold fast to what is good" (Rom. 12:9*b*).

As you look at this big piece of white poster board, tell me what you see. A spot? A smudge? I was afraid you were going to say that. Surely you can be more positive.

Here is what I see. A nice, big sheet of poster board which is practically new and unblemished. Except for one little spot, it is perfect. We could use it for many different things like making pictures or signs. But you saw only the bad part. That's very negative. Why are people so negative and quick to see faults?

You may wake up one day thinking, *I will be a good child all day long.* So you obey your parents, eat your vegetables, carry your dinner plate to the sink, and even make your bed. All day long you try to be the perfect child who does everything right.

Yet no one notices when you are good. Isn't that disappointing? But if you do just one little thing wrong—perhaps you leave your shoes in the hall—and *wham!* You get jumped on and corrected because it's always easier for other people to see faults rather than good deeds.

We parents ought to learn a lesson here. Be positive. We should emphasize the good. And so should you children. Don't give up being good! Always think good thoughts.

The Bible says, "Hold fast to what is good." That means to emphasize all the good habits and good thoughts. Don't give up doing good deeds. Don't get discouraged. Keep on trying to do good. Be positive.

A Better Pump

Visual Introduction: Plastic pump and hose for fuel transfer.

Sentence Summary: God made our hearts to be the best pump of all.

Scripture Text: "I will praise thee; for I am fearfully and wonderfully made" (Ps. 139:14, KJV).

If you are ever in an automobile that runs out of gas, then here is a handy little pump which can be most helpful. It may be purchased from any hardware store or an auto parts place and kept for emergencies like a lack of gasoline. When someone pulls along and asks you if any help is needed, you reply: "May I pump a little gas from your car into mine?" Then you will be on your way again.

This is just one of a thousand different types of pumps designed by clever people to push or pull fluids both uphill and downhill. Big steel pumps keep water flowing through our faucets. Oil is pushed through pipelines buried in the ground. Gasoline is pulled from the fuel tank up to the engine of an automobile. Pumps are everywhere around us working hard.

But the best and strongest pump ever created is not made of plastic or steel. God designed the most marvelous pump of all, and He gave you one of them. You brought it with you today. Feel your chest for the steady beating of the best pump in the world. We call that pump a heart.

Your heart does not pump gas or water but something more important. Day and night it pumps blood around and around inside your body. It beats about 70 times a minute, 4200 times an hour, and more than 100,000 times every full day. It does that for years and years without a rest.

Some people have sick hearts that get very tired. Doctors have developed a metal heart which can pump for a few years, but nothing can really replace the heart that God first gave you. It is a wonder and a miracle. Let's thank God in the words of the psalmist who said, "I will praise thee; for I am fearfully and wonderfully made" (KJV).

Be a Friend

Visual Introduction: Plastic back scratcher or a simple stick.
Sentence Summary: Be a friend and help someone.

Scripture Text: "Do for others just what you want them to do for you" (Luke 6:31, GNB).

Have you ever had an itch you could not reach? Everyone has a little spot right in the middle of the back which just cannot be reached with these arms that God gave us.

When that happens to you, you might be interested in this little invention. It is just a stick. But look what it can do. You can use it to reach over your shoulders and scratch that little spot in your back. That feels so good.

But what if you don't have a stick to scratch your back? Then you need a friend. A friend can scratch your back even better. Then you can scratch his. What a wonderful way to treat others.

Let's do an experiment to demonstrate how we can be a friend and still get our own backs scratched. Gather around me in a circle as if you were going to march around me. Everyone must prepare to march in the same direction. That way you will have someone in front of you and someone else behind you.

Now take your hand and scratch the back of that person in front of you. That child is very happy right now. And you feel good for helping your friend in front of you.

But wait! You can also feel good for another reason. At the same time you are being a friend to someone in front of you, your back is being scratched by a friend behind you. This illustrates how Jesus wants us to be a friend to everyone. He said, "Do for others just what you want them to do for you" (GNB).

Believe in Things Not Seen

Visual Introduction: Two packets of sugar and a glass of water.

Sentence Summary: You need not see something to believe it.

Scripture Text: "Now faith is the assurance of things hoped for, the conviction of things not seen" (Heb. 11: 1).

Would you like to see a magic trick today? I promise that before your own eyes I will make the sugar in these little packets vanish. Every grain of sugar will disappear while you are watching.

Would someone bring me a glass of water? Thank you. Now watch as I pour the sugar into this water and stir it briefly. Presto! Now the sugar is gone.

Some of you are a little disappointed. I confess that this is not a very mysterious trick. Everyone knows where the sugar went. It simply dissolved in the water.

But you cannot see the sugar. How many of you really believe the sugar is still in that glass of water? Well, I am glad that all of you believe. Everyone here has faith enough to believe that the sugar is still there. Yet we do not see it. We believe by faith rather than sight.

Faith is believing in things that we cannot see. We cannot see God. Yet we know that He is here. He has promised us many wonderful things in this life and in heaven to come. Even though we cannot see those things which He has promised, we believe.

In Hebrews 11 we find a good definition of faith or

belief. "Now faith is the assurance of things hoped for, a conviction of things not seen."

So many good things which God offers us cannot be seen. We must trust God. Then we can be sure He will give us the things we hope for. We can be certain of things we do not see.

Finding God

Visual Introduction: Leader closes his eyes, turns his head, and begins counting.

Sentence Summary: Rather than hide from us, God meets us halfway.

Scripture Truth: "Draw near to God and he will draw near to you" (Jas. 4:8).

Can you guess what kind of game children all over the world enjoy playing? I will demonstrate how it begins. I close my eyes and turn around to be sure I won't see you. Then I start counting. Of course, you know what to do next. What kind of game is this? You are correct. This is hide-and-seek.

Perhaps your friends all take off running around the house and through the backyard. Then you go looking for them and can never find them. Why? Sometimes children cheat by moving around. They will not stay put. When you aren't looking, they keep moving further away. They become a moving target and impossible to find. Now that is not fair, is it? At least, not in the old-fashioned game of hide-and-seek.

Perhaps the backyard or park is very big with lots of wonderful places to hide. Then it becomes more difficult to find someone, especially if you are a small child. In that case, instead of moving away we might want to help by moving in closer. Then the child would call, "Here I come, ready or not."

And you could call back, "We are all here, and we are coming toward you." That would make it much easier for a small child.

Some people think that God is always hiding from them. Everytime they hope to get close to Him, God seems to run off hiding in some place further away. But that is not God's way. God knows when we are searching for Him, and He wants more than anything else for us to find Him. So He helps us. If we will come close to God, then He moves toward us. "Draw near to God and he will draw near to you."

No Losers with the Lord

Visual Introduction: A laurel wreath crown.

Sentence Summary: Everyone wins with God.

Scripture Text: "Henceforth there is laid up for me the crown of righteousness, which the Lord, the righteous judge, will award to me on that Day, and not only to me but also to all who have loved his appearing" (2 Tim. 4:8).

Note: You can make a winner's wreath resembling those of ancient Greece by using honeysuckle or most any green vine. Just avoid poison ivy!

Do you like my crown? This is not the crown of a king but it is like the kind awarded to athletes in ancient Greece. If a person won a long-distance race, the ruler of his country would place this crown on that winner's head.

Only one person could win a race. So only one winner's wreath was awarded. But what makes this award so different is that it is made from a green vine which will soon wilt. In a day or two this trophy will look terrible. The leaves will have turned brown and fallen off. People will soon forget that this winner ever won a race. That is because in ancient Greece they had a race nearly every day. So it was only the most recent winner who was being remembered.

That does not seem fair. Only one person could win the race. No one else got a crown but that one winner. But even then he did not remain a winner after the next race was run.

We can be glad that God gives better rewards than this wreath which will fade so soon. How wonderful that everyone wins with God. The Lord has no losers on His side.

Saint Paul looked forward to a better crown waiting for him. He called it a crown of righteousness. Listen to how he explains this crown that is to be given to everyone who loves God. "Henceforth there is laid up for me the crown of righteousness, which the Lord, the righteous judge, will award to me on that Day, and not only to me but also to all who have loved his appearing."

Index of Scripture Texts